Pure
Sunshine

Rachael

age 5

July 2002

Give pages texture and *dimension*. Untwist or coil Twistel into interesting shapes. You'll find many uses for this versatile paper yarn.

Pure Sunshine
by Kristin Dungan

White and Yellow cardstock • *EK Success* Gold plaid vellum • Daffodil Twistel • 10 assorted Yellow buttons • Yellow fiber • Orange chalk • Yellow and Black pens
Tip: Use a paper plate as a guide to draw the sun shape.

HERITAGE
PAGE
LEAF PATTERN

Fun &
Unique
Album
Accents!

1. Wrap Twistel around a dowel or crochet needle.

2. Remove coiled Twistel from dowel. Pull and stretch coils.

3. Glue Twistel on page.

4. Twistel can be untwisted and glued on page.

Heritage Page
by Delores Frantz

Cardstock (Metallic Gold, Moss Green, Green, *Keeping Memories Alive* Dark Lilac flecks) • *Design Originals* Yellow stripe paper • Vellum • Willow Twistel • *Making Memories* 3/8" and 1/2" Berry buttons • 27" of 1" Pale Gold wire edge chiffon ribbon • 1/8" dowel • 4 Gold eyelets • Eyelet setter • 1/8" circle punch • *Sizzix* die cutter • 2" leaf die • Edwardian script computer font

Andrew and Mary Parker

Buttons

Buttons, Buttons, Buttons… Gather your own collection or use those wonderful buttons your grandma saved to add color and visual interest to pages and borders. You can use buttons to outline, to make flower centers, to construct wheels or to accent designs. Just let your imagination soar!

Cute as a Button Page
by Delores Frantz

White and Pink cardstock • Spring Green dot paper • Vellum • 17 assorted ⅝" pastel buttons • Scallop and clouds scissors • *Creating Keepsakes* Anything Goes font • Dark Green chalk

TIP: Print title across top and name across bottom of a full sheet of vellum. Cut edges with cloud scissors. Apply chalk to edges. Print date on White cardstock. Cut heart around the date using pattern.

Button Flowers
by Stephanie Barnard

White cardstock • Pink dot paper and *Sweetwater Scrapbook* Yellow print • Pink and Yellow chenille stems • Pink and Yellow embroidery floss • Five ¾" White buttons • Needle

TIP: Using pattern as guide, form petals of flower. Secure petals together with button and floss. Anchor to paper with floss.

CHENILLE STEM FLOWER PATTERN

Cute As A Button

Kaitlyn - 6 Months

April 2002

Button & Bows Border
by Stephanie Barnard

Yellow and Blue cardstock • *Sweetwater Scrapbook* Yellow and Blue check paper • Light Blue embroidery floss • 1" square punch • Needle

TIPS: Attach buttons with floss. Sew small stitch through paper and tie floss bows.

Fun at the Zoo
by Delores Frantz

Cardstock (Deep Red, Black, Blue, Gray, Pink, Yellow, Brown, Light Gold, Dark Gold, Rust) • *Design Originals* Blue ticking stripe paper • Buttons (3 Red $7/8$", 4 Blue $7/8$", 1 Red $3/4$" and 3 Blue $5/16$") • Deckle and stamp scissors • Circle punches ($1\frac{1}{4}$", 1", $3/4$", $5/8$", $1/2$", $5/16$", $1/4$", $1/8$") • Heart punches ($1\frac{1}{4}$", $3/4$", $3/8$") • $5/8$" punches (oval, spiral, sun) • *Sizzix* die cutter • Alphabet and train dies

TIPS: Cut 2 train cars $2\frac{1}{2}$" x $13/16$". Cut the right side of the Giraffe mane using deckle scissors.

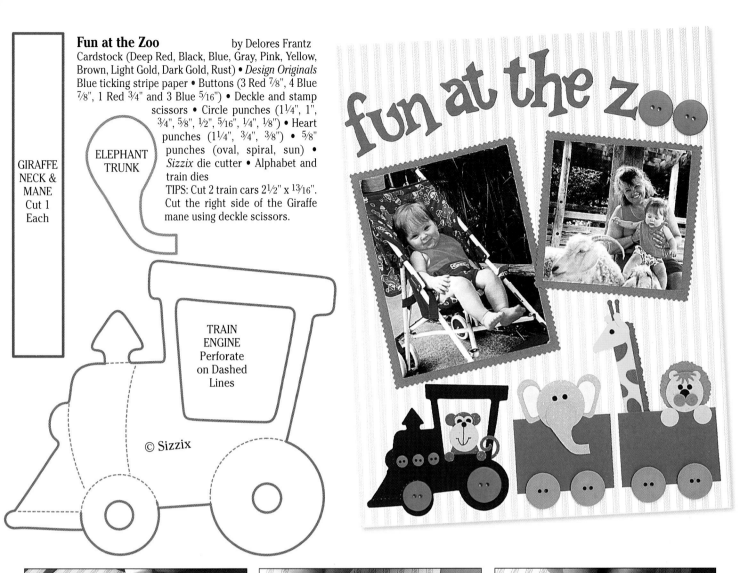

GIRAFFE NECK & MANE
Cut 1 Each

ELEPHANT TRUNK

TRAIN ENGINE
Perforate on Dashed Lines

© Sizzix

1. Glue buttons on the page.
2. To tie buttons on page, thread needle with 6 strands of floss. Position button on page. Push needle and floss down thru one button hole and page leaving 1" tail. Bring needle up through page and second button hole. Cut floss leaving 1" tail. Tie tails in a knot.
3. Use needle and 3 strands of floss to sew buttons to page or cardstock.

Spring
by Stephanie Barnard

Sweetwater Scrapbook paper (Blue, Pink, Green, Lavender, Yellow print) • 3 Yellow $3/8$" buttons • Yellow embroidery floss • *Accu-Cut* flower and leaf die-cuts • Needle

SNOWFLAKE STITCHING PATTERN

Tahoe
by Delores Frantz

Cardstock (White, Blue, Forest Green) • Silver and Green Metallic embroidery floss • 25 Dark Green eyelets • *Sizzix* die cutter • Large and medium pine tree dies • 1/8" hole punch • Needle

TIP: Cut and glue White trees behind Green trees to give the effect of snow on the branches.

1. Mark eyelet placement. Using cutting mat, 1/8" punch and hammer, punch holes in page or cardstock.

2. Insert eyelets from front to back. Place eyelet and cardstock face down on mat. Position eyelet setting tool on top of eyelet and hit with hammer.

3. Thread needle with 6 strands of floss or stiffen ends with glue. Thread through eyelets to form letters or design. Attach ends to back of page with tape or glue.

4. Transfer stitch pattern. Punch holes with pin. Thread needle with 3 strands of floss. Stitch through holes. Tape or glue ends on back of page.

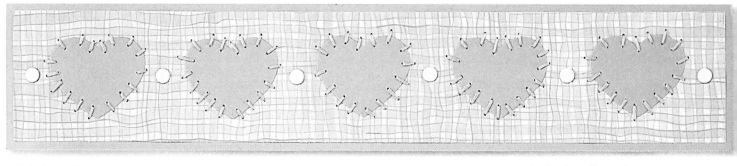

Stitched Hearts
by Stephanie Barnard

Lavender cardstock • *Carolee's Creations* Pink plaid paper • 6 White 1/4" brads • Pink embroidery floss • *Accu-Cut* die-cut hearts • Needle

• Floss & Jute •

It is so much fun to add floss and jute to scrapbook pages. Make holes in the paper and insert eyelets if you wish and sew the design. Or you can draw a design with pencil, add glue and press jute in place. Whatever method you choose, you'll love the results.

Write letters or draw design on page or cardstock with pencil. Trace with White glue and toothpick. Press jute or string into glue.

Wild West by Delores Frantz
Cardstock (Rust, Light Gold, Dark Gold, Brown Kraft) • 72" of jute • 4" of Rust cotton crochet thread • 2 Silver ⅜" brads • 6 Green and 4 Blue E beads • Deckle scissors • Brown chalk • Black gel pen • White glue

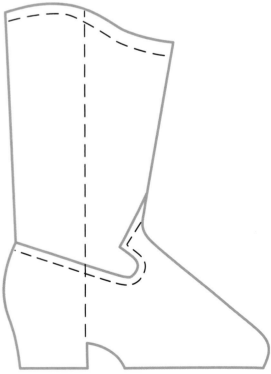

At the Park by Stephanie Barnard
Cardstock (White, Red, Pale Blue, Yellow) • Twistel (Red, Natural, Pine) • 6 Red ¼" brads • Jute • Gold and Iridescent glitter glue • *Accu-Cut* die cuts (grass, sun, clouds, letters, tree)
Park patterns are on pages 10 and 11.

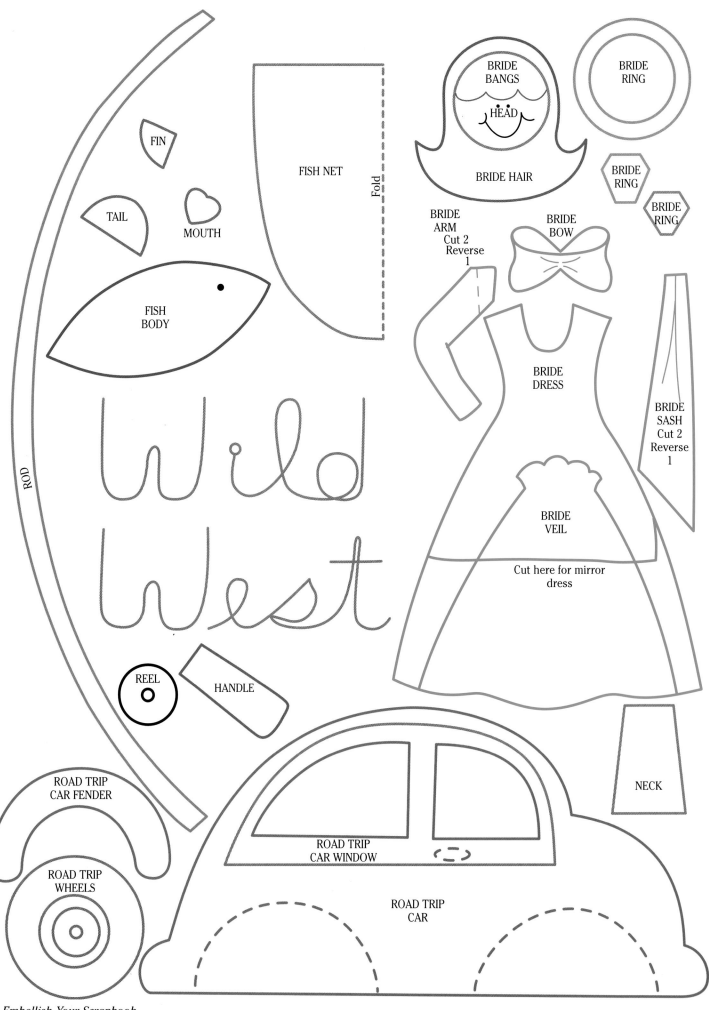

FIN

TAIL

MOUTH

FISH NET

Fold

FISH BODY

ROD

Wild West

REEL

HANDLE

BRIDE BANGS

HEAD

BRIDE HAIR

BRIDE RING

BRIDE RING

BRIDE RING

BRIDE ARM
Cut 2
Reverse
1

BRIDE BOW

BRIDE DRESS

BRIDE SASH
Cut 2
Reverse
1

BRIDE VEIL

Cut here for mirror dress

NECK

ROAD TRIP CAR FENDER

ROAD TRIP WHEELS

ROAD TRIP CAR WINDOW

ROAD TRIP CAR

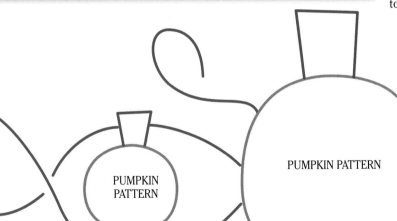

Fibers are Fun! Wrap them around borders for a colorful display or drape them across a page to create swags. Glue them in a solid pattern for flowers and leaves. Or add the creepy to your crawlies with webs and fuzzy legs. Sew designs, highlight titles, tie bows. Fibers will fill your pages with inspired color and unusual texture.

Grand Ole Pumpkin Patch   by Susan Bascom

Cardstock (Light Green, Green, Lime Green) • Gold vellum • 4 *Scrapadoodledoo.com* ¼" Green eyelets • Green yarn • *Fibersbytheyard.com* Orange fibers • Eyelet setter • ⅛" hole punch • *Creating Keepsakes* pumpkin patch font • White gel pen • Glue dots • Glue pen

TIPS: Lightly draw pumpkins on paper leaving space for stems. For small pumpkins, fill in outline with glue dots and wind fiber on top working from center out. For large pumpkin, fill in line drawing with glue one line at a time and tap fiber into glue. Add vines with glue dots and stems with glue.

FALL FUN
PUMPKIN BEADING
DIAGRAM

Pull wire taut as you go, twist wire at the end and tuck behind pumpkin.

Seed beads vary in size, use as many or few as needed to fit pumpkin pattern.

PUMPKIN PATTERN

PUMPKIN PATTERN

PUMPKIN PATTERN

Fall Fun
by Stephanie Barnard

Gold and Dark Gold cardstock • *Sweetwater Gold* plaid paper • Orange and Green 26 gauge wire • Orange and Green seed beads • Wire cutters • Brown and Green markers

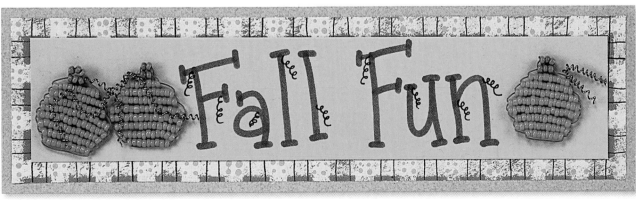

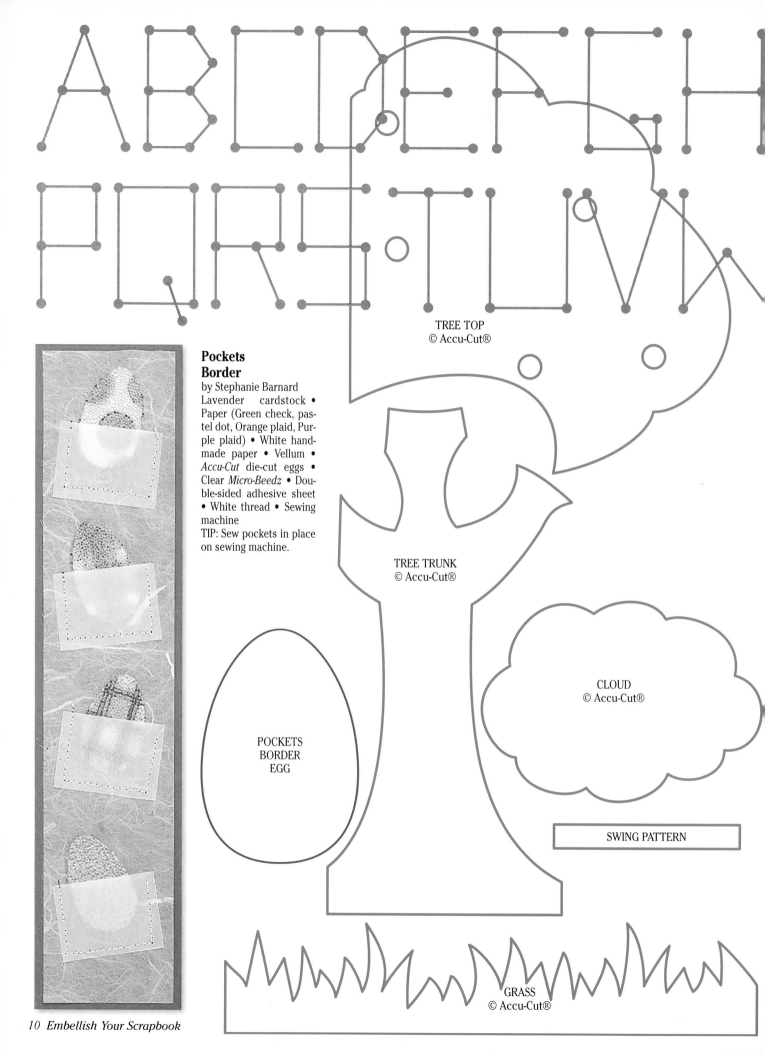

ABCDEFGH
PQRSTUVW

**Pockets
Border**
by Stephanie Barnard
Lavender cardstock •
Paper (Green check, pastel dot, Orange plaid, Purple plaid) • White handmade paper • Vellum •
Accu-Cut die-cut eggs •
Clear *Micro-Beedz* • Double-sided adhesive sheet
• White thread • Sewing machine
TIP: Sew pockets in place on sewing machine.

TREE TOP
© Accu-Cut®

TREE TRUNK
© Accu-Cut®

CLOUD
© Accu-Cut®

POCKETS
BORDER
EGG

SWING PATTERN

GRASS
© Accu-Cut®

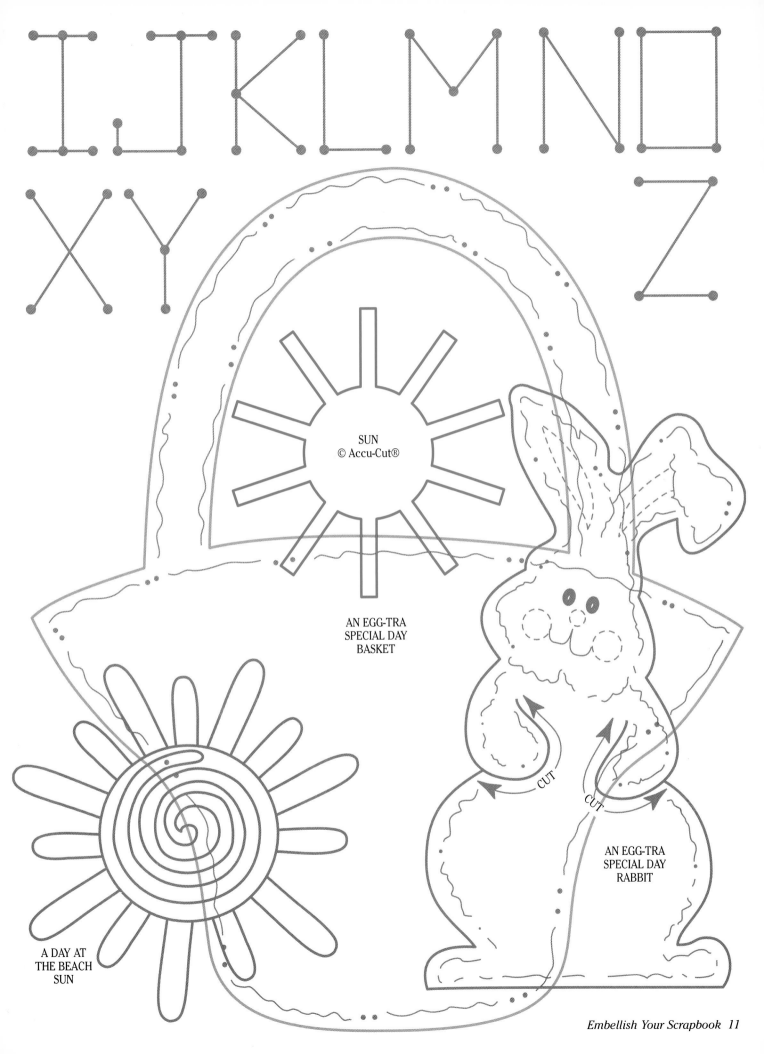

SUN
© Accu-Cut®

AN EGG-TRA
SPECIAL DAY
BASKET

AN EGG-TRA
SPECIAL DAY
RABBIT

CUT

CUT

A DAY AT
THE BEACH
SUN

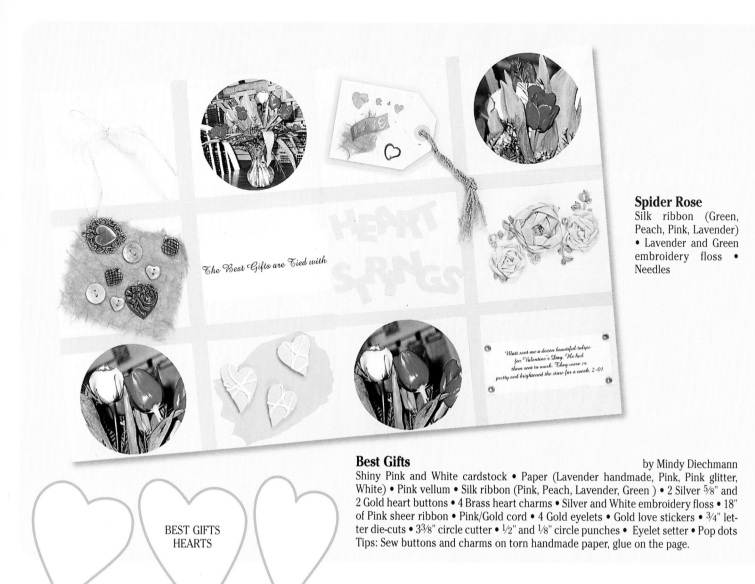

Spider Rose
Silk ribbon (Green, Peach, Pink, Lavender) • Lavender and Green embroidery floss • Needles

The Best Gifts are Tied with

BEST GIFTS
HEARTS

Best Gifts
by Mindy Diechmann

Shiny Pink and White cardstock • Paper (Lavender handmade, Pink, Pink glitter, White) • Pink vellum • Silk ribbon (Pink, Peach, Lavender, Green) • 2 Silver $5/8$" and 2 Gold heart buttons • 4 Brass heart charms • Silver and White embroidery floss • 18" of Pink sheer ribbon • Pink/Gold cord • 4 Gold eyelets • Gold love stickers • $3/4$" letter die-cuts • $3\frac{3}{8}$" circle cutter • $1/2$" and $1/8$" circle punches • Eyelet setter • Pop dots
Tips: Sew buttons and charms on torn handmade paper, glue on the page.

Star Boxes
by Mindy Deichmann

Bazzill Basics Light Blue and Dark Blue cardstock • Paper (*Reynolds* Copper foil, *Magenta* Blue net, Blue shimmer, *Solum World* Dark Blue wavy corrugated, White, *Paper Adventures* Dark Blue velvet, Copper crinkle) • Vellum • Copper ink pad • *AMACO* Copper metal mesh • Copper wire • *Magic Scraps* sea glass • Assorted embroidery floss • Blue fibers • *JudiKins* Copper Rox • 3 *Magic Scraps* tiny Blue buttons • Paper crimper • Decorative scissors • Wire cutters • *All Night Media* pop dots • Computer generated words
Tip: Cut background squares for stars $2\frac{1}{8}$" x $2\frac{1}{2}$".

STARS

SPIDER ROSE TAGS
PATTERNS

Spider Rose

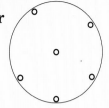

1. Sketch circle and punch holes for ribbon.

2. Make 5 long stitches from center with floss.

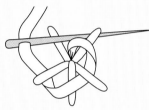

3. Weave over and under long stitches with ribbon. Let ribbon twist, do not pull tight.

Lazy Daisy Stitch - Bring needle up from back, hold ribbon down with thumb and insert needle ⅛" from starting point. Pass needle over ribbon and make a small holding stitch.

A few simple stitches and beautiful silk ribbon can turn your designs into works of art. Three- dimensional flowers and plants add depth and opulence!

Joy Page
by Mindy Deichmann
Bazzill Basics vellum and Metallic Gold cardstock • Green and Pink silk ribbon • Tan embroidery floss • Assorted *Adornaments* fibers • *Embellish it!* Brass Christmas charms • *Blue Moon* assorted seed beads • Gold leaf • Leaf adhesive • Computer generated journaling

JOY TREE PATTERN

JOY FLOWER PATTERN

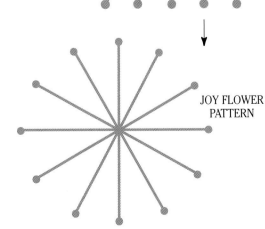

1. Cut 5" of wire edge sheer ribbon. Paint cut ribbon ends with clear nail polish or Fray Check. Grasp and pull wire ends on one side of ribbon and tightly gather ribbon.

2. Twist wire together to secure. Shape into a circle. Glue button in center of circle. Glue Green twistel for stem.

3. Cut 4" strips of Green ribbon. Following diagram, fold strip into leaves. Tightly gather center of leaves with needle and thread. Glue leaves on stem.

Grandkids
by Delores Frantz
Design Originals
Blue stripe paper • Blue polka dot paper • Vellum • 5/8" wire edge sheer ribbon (10" of Red, 10" of Blue, 5" of Yellow, 20" of Green) • 15 " of Lime Green Twistel • 5 Yellow 7/16" buttons • 4 Navy Blue eyelets • Eyelet setter • 1/8" hole punch • Clear nail polish • Needle and thread • *Creating Keepsakes* frosting font

Leaf Illustrations

1. Cut and fold leaf strip.

GRANDKIDS LEAF PATTERN

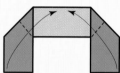

2. Fold the ends up and over.

3. Your leaf will look like this. Tightly gather the center of leaf

Hanging Hearts
by Stephanie Barnard
Blue and Yellow cardstock • *Magic Mesh* Blue mesh • 3 *Jewel-Craft* Silver nailheads • 1½ yards of 1/8" White satin ribbon • *Accu-Cut* die-cut hearts • 1/8" hole punch • Black permanent pen

faith

hope

love

HEART PATTERN © Accu-Cut®

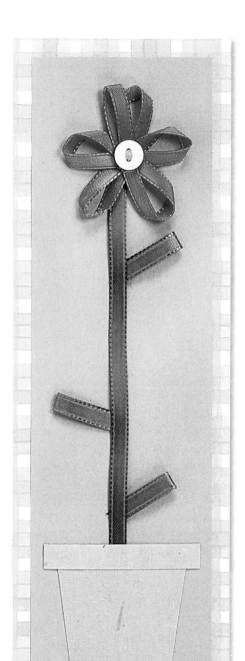

Ribbon is a quick and easy way to decorate album pages. Fold, gather, tie or wrap… the results are spectacular! Add ribbon roses for even more fun.

Mom
by Debby Schuh

K and Company Cream embossed cardstock • *Anna Griffin* Pink paper • *Hot Off he Press* papers (Light Moss Green, Dark Moss Green, Brown) • One yard of $3/8$" Ivory sheer ribbon • 8 Pink ribbon roses • 4 *Dress-It-Up!* Ivory $1/2$" buttons • Punches (3" circle, $2^1/2$" circle, 2" circle, $5/8$" circle, $7/8$" ivy leaf) • $2^1/4$" letter template • Craft knife • *Creating Keepsakes* script font

FLOWERPOT

Flowerpot
by Stephanie Barnard

Pink and Pale Green cardstock • Pink check paper • Green and Pink $1/4$" satin ribbon • $3/8$" White button • Pink embroidery floss • Needle

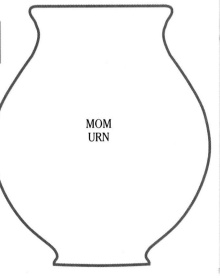

MOM URN

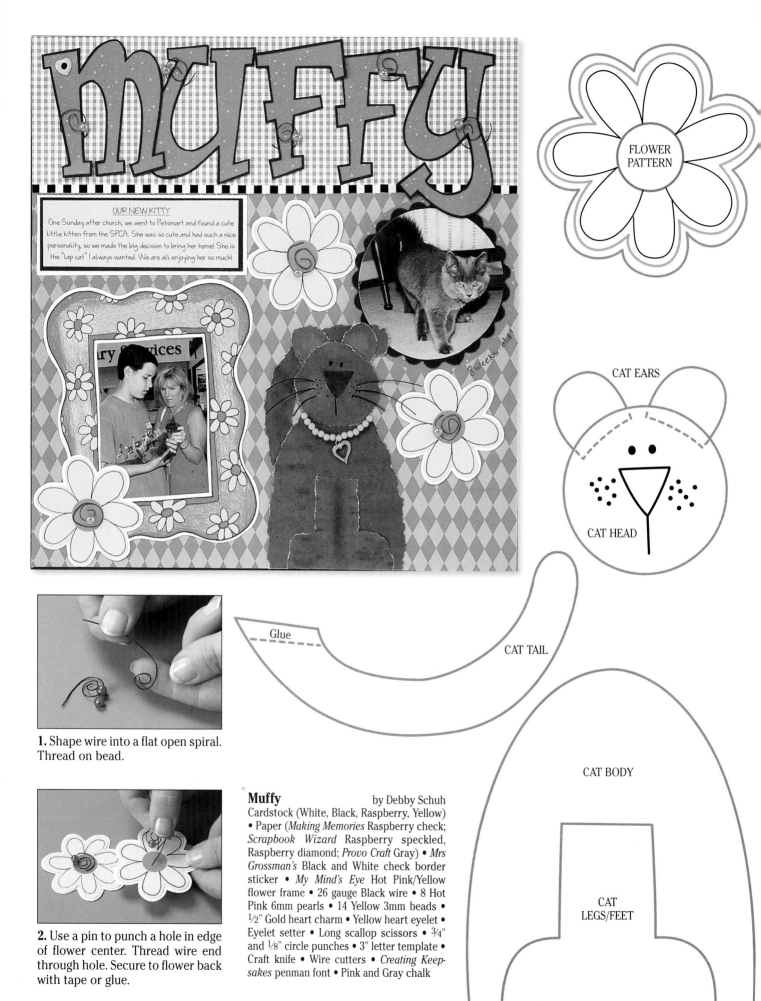

FLOWER PATTERN

OUR NEW KITTY
One Sunday after church, we went to Petsmart and found a cute little kitten from the SPCA. She was so cute and had such a nice personality, so we made the big decision to bring her home! She is the "lap cat" I always wanted. We are all enjoying her so much!

8 weeks old!

CAT EARS

CAT HEAD

CAT TAIL

Glue

CAT BODY

CAT LEGS/FEET

1. Shape wire into a flat open spiral. Thread on bead.

2. Use a pin to punch a hole in edge of flower center. Thread wire end through hole. Secure to flower back with tape or glue.

Muffy by Debby Schuh
Cardstock (White, Black, Raspberry, Yellow) • Paper (*Making Memories* Raspberry check; *Scrapbook Wizard* Raspberry speckled, Raspberry diamond; *Provo Craft* Gray) • *Mrs Grossman's* Black and White check border sticker • *My Mind's Eye* Hot Pink/Yellow flower frame • 26 gauge Black wire • 8 Hot Pink 6mm pearls • 14 Yellow 3mm beads • ½" Gold heart charm • Yellow heart eyelet • Eyelet setter • Long scallop scissors • ¾" and ⅛" circle punches • 3" letter template • Craft knife • Wire cutters • *Creating Keepsakes* penman font • Pink and Gray chalk

HAPPY
BUTTERFLY

Sparkle & shine are yours... string beads on wire, twist the wire into interesting shapes.

Happy
by Delores Frantz

Cardstock (Yellow, Blue, Red, Green) • *Design Originals* Blue cloud paper • Die cuts (Green grass, Blue butterfly, Red butterfly, Red HAPPY) • 10 Red eyelets • 3 Yellow flower eyelets • Eyelet setter • Punches (2" flower, 1" flower, ¾" heart, ⅝" spiral, ⅛" circle)

TIP: Cut ¾" punched hearts in half to make leaves and trim on butterfly wings.

HAPPY FLOWER

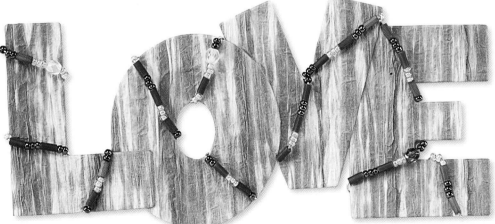

Love
by Stephanie Barnard

Pink cardstock • Berry Twistel • *Accu-Cut* die cut letters • 26 gauge Silver wire • Assorted beads • Wire cutters

TIP: String beads on wire and wrap around letters.

Beads add luster and shine to borders and titles. You won't believe how quick it is to achieve such stunning results.

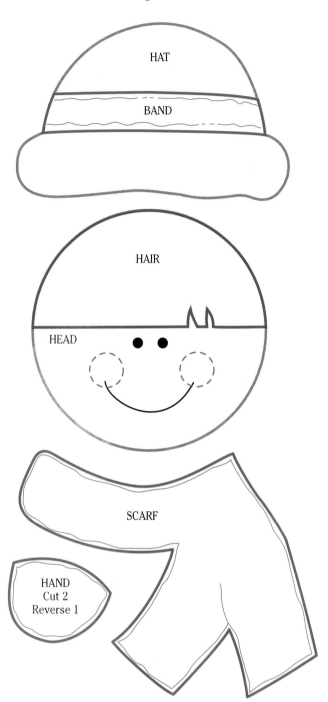

HAT

BAND

HAIR

HEAD

SCARF

HAND
Cut 2
Reverse 1

Baby Becky   by Delores Frantz
Cardstock (White, Pale Green) • *Design Originals* Pink check paper • *K & Company* baby embossed paper • Vellum • 36" of pastel fiber • Wire • 14 Hot Pink 4mm beads • Alphabet beads • 6 Pink flower eyelets • Scallop scissors • 1/8" and 1/16" circle punches • Wire cutters • Eyelet setter • Park Avenue computer font

Winter Wonder   by Debby Schuh
Cardstock (White, Blue, Red, Brown, Peach, Black) • Paper (*Provo Craft* Yellow sponged and Blue plaid, *Making Memories* White with Blue dot and White swirl embossed) • Clear *Micro-Beedz* • Assorted Blue beads • Dark Blue rocheille beads • 26 gauge Silver and Dark Blue wire • 1/2" White pompom • 1" and 2" letter templates • 2" and 1" snowflake punches • Craft knife • Deckle scissors • Wire cutters • Pop dots • Double sided adhesive sheet • Pink chalk • Black gel pen

1. String beads on 18" of wire leaving 4" or 5" of bare wire. Using pattern as a guide, form first loop. Twist wire together under loop.

2. Form second loop aligned with first loop. Wrap wire around center once. Continue adding 4 more loops. Glue rhinestone on flower center.

3. Position flower on page. Punch a hole in page at the end of each petal with a pin. Use a needle and thread to secure each petal to page. Using pattern as a guide, shape letters twisting wire once where wire crosses beads.

Beaded Flowers
by Delores Frantz
Pink and Red seed beads • 4mm Red faceted bead • 28 gauge wire • Old scissors or wire cutters

LARGE 6 PETAL FLOWER PATTERN

Love at First Sight
by Delores Frantz
Blue cardstock • *Provo Craft* Blue paper • Blue vellum • 14" of 1½" Pale Blue chiffon ribbon • 3 Dark Blue and 8 Aqua 6mm rhinestones • Assorted Blue and Green rocheille beads • 26 gauge Aqua wire • Needle and thread • Scallop scissors • Wire cutters • Park Avenue computer font

Love
by Stephanie Barnard
Pink and Dark Pink cardstock • Red bugle beads • Pink seed beads • 28 gauge Silver wire • Wire cutters • Needle and thread

BEADING PATTERN

SMALL HEART PATTERN

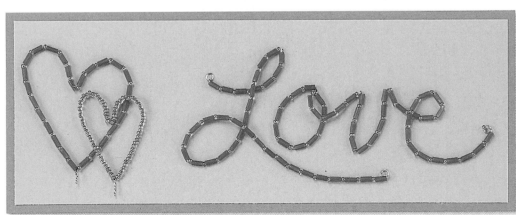

Fasteners

Eyelets and brads are a versatile addition to any page and are available in a variety of colors and shapes. Use them to attach components, make flowers and leaves or emphasize the page theme.

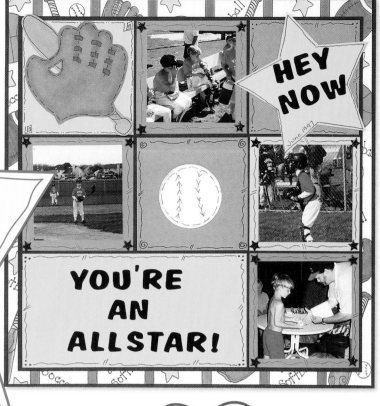

You're an Allstar
by Debby Schuh

Cardstock (Black, Yellow, Orange, Blue, White, Brown, Tan) • *Design Originals* Sports paper • 16 Black star eyelets • Eyelet setter • 2" and ⅛" circle punches • ⅝" Black letter stickers • Black and Brown chalk • Red and Black pens

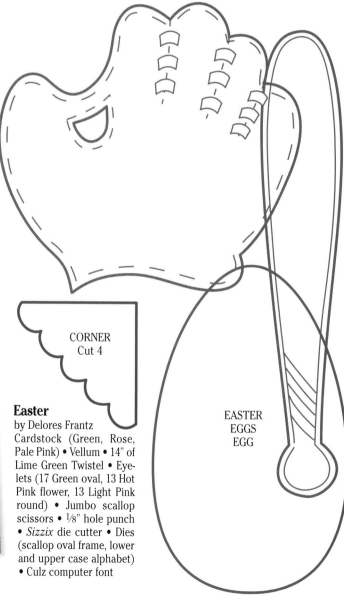

CORNER
Cut 4

EASTER
EGGS
EGG

Easter
by Delores Frantz

Cardstock (Green, Rose, Pale Pink) • Vellum • 14" of Lime Green Twistel • Eyelets (17 Green oval, 13 Hot Pink flower, 13 Light Pink round) • Jumbo scallop scissors • ⅛" hole punch • *Sizzix* die cutter • Dies (scallop oval frame, lower and upper case alphabet) • Culz computer font

WRENCH

HAMMER

SCREW
DRIVER

SAW
BLADE

PUMPKIN PATTERN
© Accu-Cut®

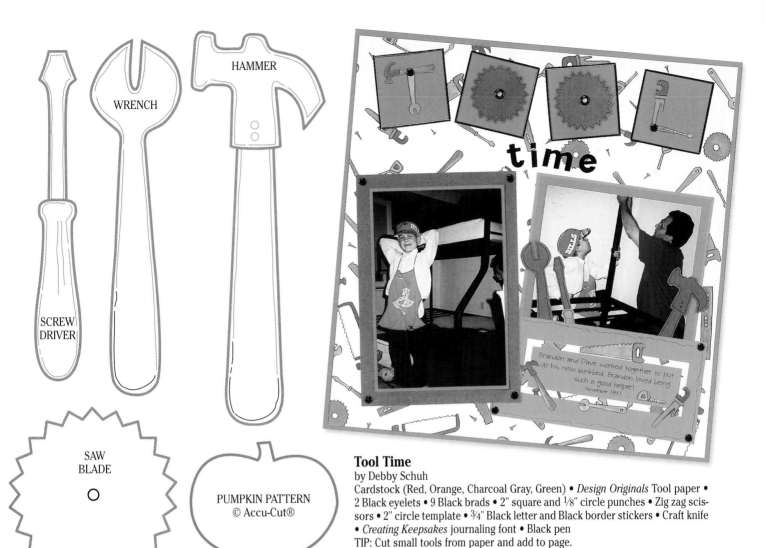

Tool Time
by Debby Schuh
Cardstock (Red, Orange, Charcoal Gray, Green) • *Design Originals* Tool paper •
2 Black eyelets • 9 Black brads • 2" square and ⅛" circle punches • Zig zag scissors • 2" circle template • ¾" Black letter and Black border stickers • Craft knife
• *Creating Keepsakes* journaling font • Black pen
TIP: Cut small tools from paper and add to page.

Happy Harvest
by Stephanie Barnard
Cardstock (Tan, Brown,
Orange) • Natural Twistel
• *Accu-Cut* pumpkin die-
cuts • 8 Green oval eyelets
• ⅝" Black letter stickers •
Clear *Micro-Beedz* • Double-sided adhesive sheet •
⅛" hole punch

Eggs
by Stephanie Barnard
White cardstock • Twistel
(Lavender, Daffodil, Berry,
Ocean, Spruce) • Five
9mm mirrors • 4 Green and
2 Pink 7mm x 15mm gems
• 5 Silver nailheads • Eyelets (5 White round, 2 Pink
flower, 2 Yellow flower) •
Blue bugle beads • Dark
Blue seed beads • 28 gauge
Silver wire • ⅛" hole
punch • Eyelet setter •
Wire cutters

Mesh adds that ultra important item to sports pages… nets! Or cover designs with mesh. It will add a unique touch to plain paper titles and die-cut shapes.

Fishin' by Delores Frantz
Cardstock (Brown, Black, Gray, Tan, Kelly Green, Lime Green) • *Provo Craft* Blue paper • Medium Blue Vellum • *Avant' Card* Gray Magic Mesh • 48" of Black cotton crochet thread • *Provo Craft* log letter stickers • 7 Gold eyelets • Cloud and deckle scissors • Punches (3/8" heart, 3/4" circle, 5/8" circle, 1/8" circle) • Eyelet setter

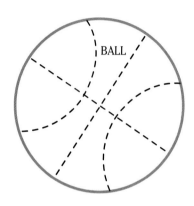

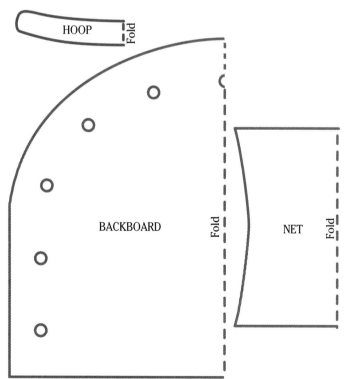

One on One by Delores Frantz
Cardstock (Rust, Tan, Brown, Royal Blue) • *Design Originals* tiny stars on Red paper • *Avant' Card* Tan Magic Mesh • 9 White star eyelets • *Making Memories* Navy Blue 1/2" letter stickers • 1/8" hole punch • Stamp scissors • *Sizzix* die cutter • Letter and number dies • Eyelet setter
TIPS: Cut mesh on the diagonal. Cut one set of Blue and one of Tan letters.

NET

NET HANDLE

Mesh is a fun way to embellish your memories!

BUTTERFLY

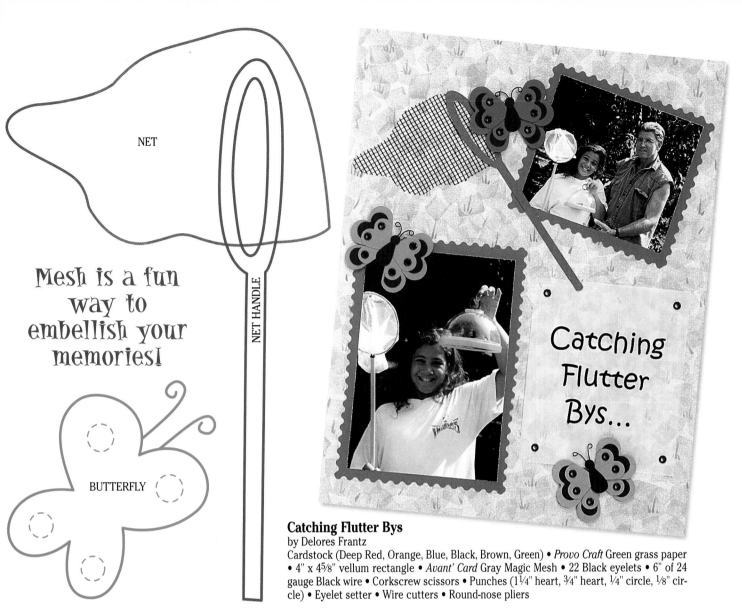

Catching Flutter Bys
by Delores Frantz
Cardstock (Deep Red, Orange, Blue, Black, Brown, Green) • *Provo Craft* Green grass paper • 4" x 4⅝" vellum rectangle • *Avant' Card* Gray Magic Mesh • 22 Black eyelets • 6" of 24 gauge Black wire • Corkscrew scissors • Punches (1¼" heart, ¾" heart, ¼" circle, ⅛" circle) • Eyelet setter • Wire cutters • Round-nose pliers

Butterflies
by Stephanie Barnard
Cardstock (Pink, Blue, Yellow, Lavender) • *Avant' Card* Pink and White Magic Mesh • Rhinestones (two 4mm Clear, two 6mm Clear, two 4mm Gold, two 6mm Gold, two 4mm Purple, two 6mm Purple) • 24 gauge Silver wire • Wire cutters • Round-nose pliers • Glitter gel pen

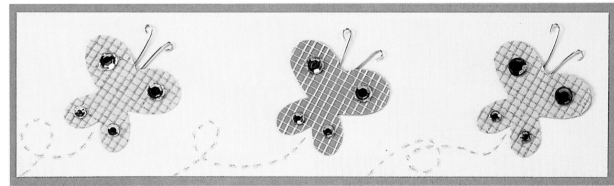

July
by Stephanie Barnard
Red cardstock • Blue and Blue print paper • *Avant' Card* Red Magic Mesh • Seed beads (Red, Clear, Blue) • 26 gauge Blue wire • *Accu-Cut* die-cut letters • Needle and thread • Wire cutters • Black permanent pen

ACCORDION FOLD BOOK DIAGRAM

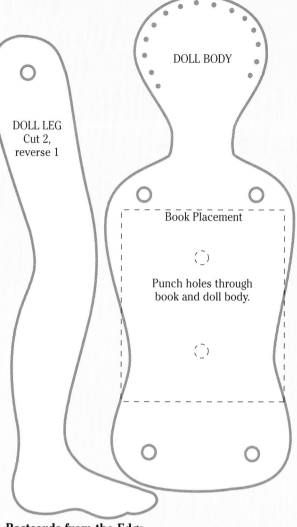

DOLL BODY

DOLL LEG
Cut 2,
reverse 1

Book Placement

Punch holes through
book and doll body.

Postcards from the Edge
by Brooke Bready for ScrapYard 329
Cardstock (Green, Gold, Black) • Postcards • *ScrapYard* Gold wire mesh • 7 Brass mini brads • 6 Gold eyelets • Assorted *Adornaments* fibers • Silver E bead • Gold gel pen • 1/8" hole punch • Eyelet setter
TIPS: Accordion fold book and punch holes through center. Attach book to doll by threading fibers through eyelets in doll. Close book with a bead.

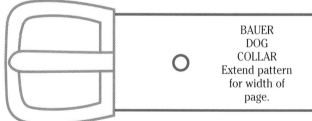

BAUER
DOG
COLLAR
Extend pattern
for width of
page.

Bauer
by Amy Harrison for ScrapYard 329
Cardstock (Dark Red, Black, Brown, White, Beige, Metallic Silver) • *ScrapYard* Black wire mesh • 5 Silver and 5 Red eyelets • *ScrapYard* aluminum studs (7 Silver 6mm, Silver 10mm, 4 Black 6mm) • 28 gauge Silver wire • Punches (5/8" bone, 5/8" paw print, 1/8" circle) • 1 1/2" letter template • Wire cutters • Craft knife • Eyelet setter • Foam tape
TIPS: Cut letters in cardstock. Attach narrow strips of foam tape to edges of mesh. Attach mesh to page inserting punched bones before pressing mesh and cardstock firmly in place.

Give a new look to your album pages!

DOLL ARM
Cut 2,
reverse 1

our little
Pumkin

Grant loves picking out pumkins. He always picks the larg est one he can find. His favorite part is carving them and eating the toasted seeds.

october 1999

Cages, pockets, back-grounds… all are fantastic when made with metal mesh. Just cut to shape and attach with thread or brads. What could be easier?

PUMPKIN

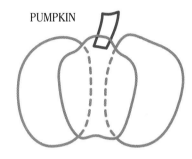

Pumpkin
by Amy Harrison for ScrapYard 329
Cardstock (Gold, Rust, Green) • *ScrapYard* Silver wire mesh • *ScrapYard* Rust heart aluminum studs • 1½" letter template • Craft knife • Brown chalk • Black permanent pen
Tip: Overlap pieces to make pumpkin.

1. Attach mesh to paper with brads or by tying with fibers.

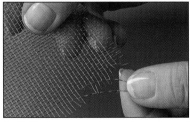

2. Pull the wires from the edge of mesh to ravel.

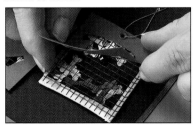

3. Attach mesh and die cut letter with foam tape.

Halloween

october 2000

Halloween
by Amy Harrison for ScrapYard 329
Cardstock (Black, White, Rust) • *ScrapYard* Black wire mesh • *Adornments* Black and Orange fibers • Assorted shapes of *ScrapYard* aluminum studs (Black, Gold, Rust) • Brown chalk • Black marker

To Read is to Dream
by Debby Schuh

Deep Red and Cream cardstock • *Design Originals* paper (sky/cloud, heritage nursery rhymes) • Red plaid paper • Vellum • Natural string • 4 Red $\frac{1}{4}$" and 8 Sage Green $\frac{5}{16}$" eyelets • Eyelet setter • $\frac{5}{8}$" flower and $\frac{1}{8}$" circle punches • $1\frac{3}{4}$" letter template • Craft knife • Pop dots • Tan chalk • Black pen

TIP: Age sky and cloud paper with Tan chalk.

TO DREAM TAG

Tags make great pages really special.

Yee Haw
by Stephanie Barnard

Cardstock (Gold, Brown, Brown Craft) • Ivory $1\frac{5}{8}$" x $3\frac{1}{4}$" tag • Jute • Paper crimper • 2 Black eyelets • Eyelet setter • *Curlz* MT computer font • Punches ($\frac{1}{2}$" circle, $\frac{1}{4}$" circle, $\frac{1}{8}$" circle)

Love
by Kristin Dungan

Paper Adventures cardstock (Gold textured, Ivory, Burgundy) • *Colors by Design* Rose leaf paper • 4 Natural $1\frac{5}{8}$" x $3\frac{1}{4}$" tags • Burgundy fiber • *Scrap Pagerz* $1\frac{5}{8}$" calligraphy letter template • Craft knife • $\frac{1}{8}$" circle punch • *Creating Keepsakes* cursive font • Tan chalk

Tags

Decorate tags with themed paper, punched letters, journaling or die-cut shapes. Hang them from your page designs for terrific results every time.

PATRIOTIC TAG

Micah

by Delores Frantz

Cardstock (White, Black, Deep Red) • *Keeping Memories Alive* Red wool plaid paper • 5 *DMD* 1⅝" x 3¼" White tags • 24" of heavy Black cotton crochet thread • 5 White eyelets • Punches (½" heart, ¼" circle, ⅛" circle) • *Sizzix* die cutter • Lower case alphabet dies

TIPS: Cut letters in tags with die cutter and make paw prints with circle and heart punches.

1. Punch the shapes or cut letters in tags with a Sizzix Die Cutter or cut using a template and craft knife. Attach to page so background paper will shows through.

2. Decorate tags with punched shapes, cut-out designs, letters or stickers.

3. Set a large ⁵⁄₁₆" eyelet in tag hole or cover hole with a punched shape and set a small ⅛" eyelet.

4. Punch small holes or set eyelets in bottom of photo mat. Hang the tags with cord, string or fiber.

Patriotic Tags

by Stephanie Barnard

Cardstock (Red, White, Blue) • Twistel (Red, White, Blue) • Eyelets (Red, White, Blue) • Gold tinsel • Primitive star and tag die cuts • ⅛" hole punch

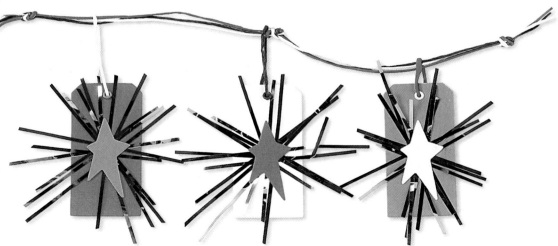

Tinsel

For glitter, glitter, glitter, tinsel is the answer. Showcase tinsel in plastic film covered openings, glue it on punched or die-cut shapes or use it for grass. It's fabulous!

JULY 4th
STARS

July 4th

Designer: Delores Frantz

Cardstock (White, Deep Red, Royal Blue) • *Design Originals* Flags on White paper • *F&M Enterprises* plastic film • Tinsel (Silver, Red, Royal Blue) • 48" of Royal Blue Twistel • Corkscrew scissors • Double-sided tape • *Sizzix* die cutter • Shadowbox alphabet dies • White glue

1. Temporarily attach flag paper to cardstock or album page. Use a craft knife to cut out star shapes cutting through both of the layers.

2. Separate paper from cardstock. Place double-sided tape around edges of opening in cardstock. Press a piece of plastic film over star opening.

3. Place a second layer of double-sided tape on the film and around star opening. Cut tinsel into small pieces and arrange on film. Press a second square of film over tinsel and tape.

4. Apply a third layer of double-sided tape on the film and around star opening. Press flag paper over cardstock matching edges of star cut-outs.

4th of July

by Stephanie Barnard

Cardstock (Red, White, Blue, Dark Blue) • Gold tinsel • *Accu-Cut* 3" star and 2" letter die-cuts • Black marker

HOME TWEET
HOME
DRAGONFLY

An Egg-Tra Special Day

by Debby Schuh

Cardstock (Yellow, Lavender, Purple, White, Green) • *Design Originals* Egg-citing Eggs paper • Green cellophane Easter grass • 2 mini and 4 large Pink flower eyelets • ¹⁄₈" hole punch • Cloud and grass scissors • ⁵⁄₈" letter template • Craft knife • Arial computer font • Pink chalk • Black pen TIP: Cut eggs from second sheet of Egg-citing paper. Basket and bunny patterns on page 15.

An Egg-tra Special Day!

Jeremy & Brandon
Easter 1998

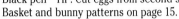

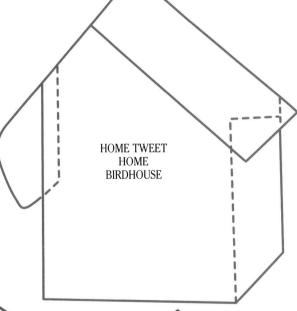

HOME TWEET
HOME
BIRDHOUSE

Home Tweet Home Page

by Michelle Guajardo for Everyone's Scrappin'

12" square of White cardstock • Paper (Green, Blue, White, Brown, Red, mirror) • *Paper Pizazz* dot vellum • Miscellaneous paper scraps • Rose and Sand Twistel • Assorted buttons (Red, Green, Blue, Magenta) • Dark Blue and Yellow embroidery floss • Green tinsel • 28 gauge Black wire • 1" letter template • Craft knife • ¹⁄₂" diamond and ¹⁄₈" circle punches • Wire cutters • Black and Brown chalk • Markers (Black, Blue, Brown, Green, Red) • *Xyron* adhesive • *Fiskars* mounting squares • Glue pen • Glue dots

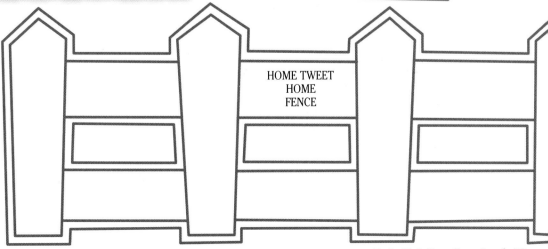

HOME TWEET
HOME
FENCE

Mackenzie
by Diane Ferree

Provo Craft paper (Pomegranate wavy plaid, White dots) • Hot Pink dots on White paper • Watermelon *Treasure Beadz* • Rose *Micro-Beedz* • Dusty Rose Sparklerz glitter • *Sizzix* die cutter • Upper and lower case alphabet dies • *Terrifically Tacky* tape sheet • *Shimmerz* glue

MACKENZIE FLOWER

A Day at the Beach
by Diane Ferree

Design Originals Blue Check and Blue Dot paper • *Provo Craft* Yellow with White dots paper • Beach stickers • *Micro-Beedz* (Gold, Sand, Autumn) • Golden Yellow *Treasure Beadz* • Sunflower scissors • *Terrifically Tacky* tape sheet • *Shimmerz* glue

Sun pattern on page 15.

Splash Time
by Diane Ferree

Turquoise cardstock • *Provo Craft* paper (Yellow wavy plaid, Yellow with White dots, Yellow checks) • Duck and splash time stickers • *Micro-Beedz* (Clear, Ocean) • Aqua seed beads • 26 gauge Blue wire • Wire cutters • Needle and thread • *Terrifically Tacky* tape sheet

SPLASH TIME PUDDLE

A DAY AT THE BEACH SHELL

A DAY AT THE BEACH SHELL

A DAY AT THE BEACH STARFISH

Glitter & Micro Beads

Glitter and beads bring your pages to a whole new dimension. Simply attach them with double-sided adhesive and glittery, shiny pizazz is yours!

LIGHT

FISH

Swim with the Fish

by Debby Schuh

Cardstock (White, Blue, Aqua) • *Design Originals* paper (Water & Swirls, Deep Blue Sea) • ½" Blue letter stickers • Aqua and Lime Green *Glitterz* • Blue and Green *Micro-Beedz & Treasure Beads* • Black brad • Eyelets (22⅛" Turquoise, two 5/16" Blue, 5/16" White) • Eyelet setter • Small paintbrush • ⅛" hole punch • Blue chalk • Black pen • *Terrifically Tacky* tape sheet • Thick White glue

TIP: Cut small fish from Deep Blue Sea paper.

1. Working on a small area at a time, paint glue on paper or cutout shapes. Sprinkle glitter on glue. Shake off excess.

2. Apply double-sided adhesive to the right side of cardstock. Trace letters or shapes on backing. Cut out letters or shapes. Peel off backing and add beads.

3. Thread beads on wire leaving 2" of bare wire. Shape beads and wire twisting wire together where it crosses.

4. Position the beads on the page. Punch a hole with a pin at each end of beads. Insert wire ends through holes. Tape or glue wire ends to wrong side of page.

Christmas Lights

by Stephanie Barnard

White cardstock • Red check paper • *Accu-Cut* light bulb die-cuts with metal bases (2 Green, Red, Yellow) • Glitter (Green, Red, Gold) • 26 gauge Black wire • Wire cutters • Needle and thread • Glitter glue

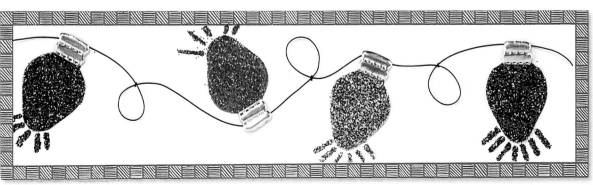

Road Trip
by Delores Frantz

Cardstock (Red, White, Black, Charcoal Gray, Yellow) • Road map paper • *Gotta Scrap Gotta Stamp* mirror paper • 3 Black eyelets • Eyelet setter • 5/8" cloud punch • Circle punches (1½", ¾", ½", ⅛") • *Sizzix* Die Cutter • *Sizzix* alphabet dies • Black chalk

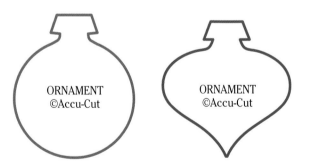

ORNAMENT
©Accu-Cut

ORNAMENT
©Accu-Cut

Wedding Day
by Delores Frantz

Cardstock (Peach, White, Medium Blue, Brown, Light Blue, Lime Green, Yellow, Rust, Metallic Gold) • Peach stripe paper • Vellum • *Gotta Scrap Gotta Stamp* mirror paper • Brass brad • Black thread • Punches (5/16" maple leaf, 5/16" flower) • Circle punches (1¼", 1", ¾", 5/16", ⅛") • Scissors (stamp, scallop) • Nuptial script computer font • Chalk (Blue, Magenta, Orange, Black, Brown) • Black gel pen. Bride patterns on page 8.

TIP: Glue punched flowers and leaves to a ¾" circle of Green cardstock. For mirror: Cut one Gold rectangle 3¼" x 5". Cut one Brown rectangle 2¾" x 4½". Cut one mirror rectangle 2¼" x 4".

Ornaments
by Stephanie Barnard

Cardstock (Dark Red, Red, Green) • *Gotta Scrap Gotta Stamp* mirror paper • Green print paper • *Accu-Cut* ornament die-cuts • Glitter (Silver, Green, Red) • 2 Silver eyelets • 24 gauge Silver wire • Wire cutters • Decorative scissors • Punches (⅛" circle, ½" star, ¼" star) • Double-sided adhesive sheet • Glitter glue

Mirror Paper

Obtain shine and metallic glow by using mirror paper for windows, jewels and shiny stars. You'll love using this reflective medium.

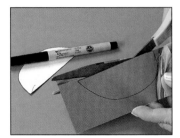

1. To cut with scissors, place pattern right side down on mirror paper. Trace pattern with permanent marker.

2. Use the ruler and craft knife to make straight cuts or use a paper cutter.

3. Use glue or double-sided tape to adhere mirror paper to album page or cardstock. Wipe fingerprints off mirror paper with a soft cloth or paper towel.

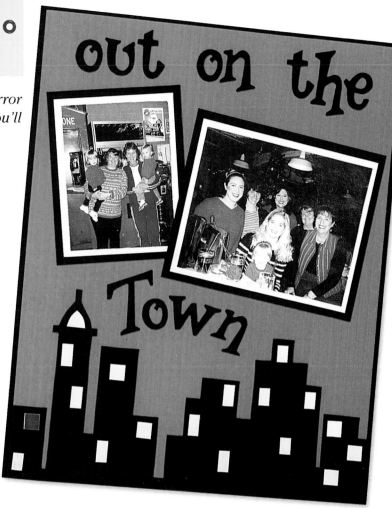

Out on the Town by Delores Frantz
Cardstock (Red embossed, Black) • *Gotta Scrap Gotta Stamp* mirror paper • *Sizzix* die cutter • Upper and lower case alphabet dies

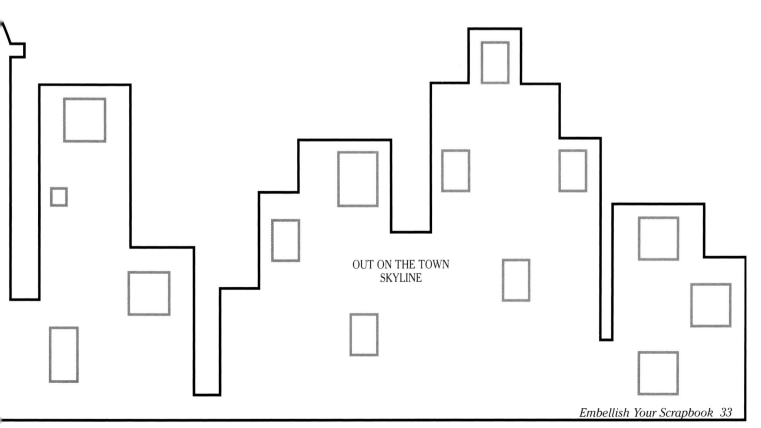

OUT ON THE TOWN
SKYLINE

MY FAVOITE THINGS

Having fun with my Mom
Going to the movies
Chewing gum
Eating Spaghetti

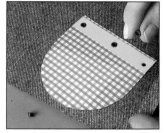
Pockets are an excellent way to display items and making them with plastic film is a snap. The film comes in rolls so you just cut to length or shape and attach with brads and eyelets!

1. Cut a pocket from Clear film and cardstock. Tape or glue side and bottom edges of the film pocket to cardstock pocket.

2. Use eyelets or brads to attach pocket to page. Fill pockets with memorabilia.

My Fav's   by Lori Ann Fowler for F&M Enterprises
Red and Yellow cardstock • *Provo Craft* plaid paper (Yellow, Orange, Red) • *Frances Meyer* denim paper • 1/8" Yellow paper ribbon • *F&M Enterprises* plastic film • 8 Black eyelets • Pocket inserts (spaghetti, ticket stubs, chewing gum) • Eyelet setter • 1/8" hole punch • 1" letter template • Craft knife • *Creating Keepsakes* journaling font

MY FAV'S
POCKET

My Blanket   by Lori Ann Fowler for F&M Enterprises
Cardstock (Yellow, Pink, Lavender) • Pink and Yellow vellum • Paper (Yellow flower, Lavender checks) • *F&M Enterprises* plastic film • 5 Purple and 8 Pink eyelets • 17 Purple 6mm beads • Alphabet beads • Scrap of fabric • Lock of hair • 26 gauge wire • Gold tinsel • 6" of Purple embroidery floss • 1" letter template • Craft knife • Wire cutters • Eyelet setter • Punches (2½" flower, 2" flower, 5/8" flower, 1/8" circle) • Purple pen